STUDIES IN EUCHARISTIC FAITH AND PRACTICE

The GALLICAN RITE

BY THE LATE

W. S. PORTER

Sometime Vicar of Colnbrook, Bucks

LO
A. R. MOWBR

THE GALLICAN RITE

STUDIES IN EUCHARISTIC FAITH AND PRACTICE

General Editor, F. L. CROSS, D.D.

The Series will comprise occasional papers on such subjects as Eucharistic theology, the history of the Eucharistic rite from the earliest times, the adjuncts of Eucharistic worship, the growth and significance of the Liturgical Movement, and modifications called for in the Eucharistic life of the Church in the conditions of the present day. It will also find a place for selected texts and documents.

STUDIES IN EUCHARISTIC FAITH AND PRACTICE

The Gallican
Rite

BY THE LATE
W. S. PORTER

Sometime Vicar of Colnbrook, Bucks.

LONDON
A. R. MOWBRAY & Co. LIMITED
NEW YORK: MOREHOUSE-GORHAM CO.

First published in 1958

PRINTED IN GREAT BRITAIN BY
A. R. MOWBRAY & CO. LIMITED IN THE CITY OF OXFORD
8315

PREFATORY NOTE

THE learned and versatile author of this paper died on February 5, 1946. In justice to his memory it should be stated that it was designed as a section in a projected work on the history and theology of the Eucharist; and that it was written some fifteen or more years ago. Thanks are due to Professor E. C. Ratcliff for his careful scrutiny of the text and the addition of one or two notes; also to the Abbot of Nashdom for permission to consult Porter's liturgical collections in the possession of Nashdom Abbey. A survey of Porter's liturgical work from the expert pen of Dom Louis Brou, O.S.B., of Quarr Abbey, will be found in *Ephemerides Liturgicae* for 1947, p. 280 f. The bibliography, which has been added for the use of students, does not derive from Porter.

F. L. CROSS

CHRIST CHURCH, OXFORD
October, 1958

CONTENTS

THE GALLICAN RITE

I

THE PROBLEMS

WHEN Augustine of Canterbury had returned to England after receiving consecration at Arles, he addressed to Pope Gregory the Great a list of questions, of which the second was this: 'Whereas the faith is one and the same, why are there different customs in different churches, and why does the Holy Roman Church celebrate Mass in one way and the Gallican in another?'

The Pope replied with good practical advice, but left the actual question unanswered.[1] No one, indeed, seriously attempted to answer it until the seventeenth century; and by that time it had become almost as difficult to say precisely what the Gallican rite had been as to explain its origins. The famous Mass of Flaccus Illyricus, published in 1557—and possibly composed by Alcuin,[2]—was issued as that which 'olim ante Romanam, circa Domini annum 700, in usu fuit,' and was widely accepted as such; but the claim collapsed as soon as genuine Gallican texts began to come to light. The chief of these were first published by Tommasi in 1680—i.e. the so-called *Missale Gothicum, Missale Gallicanum Vetus* (eighth

---

[1] Bede, *Hist. eccl.* xxvii.
[2] M.P.L. CXXXVI, 1333. Cf. F. Cabrol, *Origines liturgiques*, 1906, p. 217; but his theory of Alcuin's authorship is not convincing.

century), and *Missale Francorum* (early ninth century)—all more or less romanized.[1] Mabillon reprinted these in 1685, with the addition of the Lectionary of Luxeuil and with a learned disquisition on the whole subject of the Gallican liturgy; and in 1689 the same scholar published the *Sacramentarium Gallicanum*, now better and more properly known as the Bobbio Missal, a seventh- or eighth-century text of Celtic origin, but containing some Gallican elements.[2] In 1717 Martène published, under the title of *Expositio Brevis Antiquae Liturgiae Gallicanae*, the two letters which he had discovered a few years before at Autun, and which he attributed to Germanus, Bishop of Paris (d. 576).[3] Modern research, although it has (as we shall see) considerably altered the value and significance of these documents, has found very little to add, so far as the eucharistic rite is concerned—nothing, indeed, of any importance except the *Libellus Missarum* or small set of Masses published in 1850 by F. J. Mone, and generally known by his name.[4]

The study of this material has made it clear from the start that there was a close affinity, to say the least, between the Gallican rite and the so-called Mozarabic rite of Spain, and that their relation was part of the

[1] For modern editions, see Bibliography. Cardinal J. Bona, in *Rerum Liturgicarum libri duo*, 1671, had printed extracts from the first two, recognizing them to be Gallican.

[2] See Bibliography.

[3] In *Thesaurus novus anecdotorum*, Vol. V (M.P.L. LXXII, 83 ff.).

[4] *Lateinische u. griechische Messen aus dem zweiten bis sechsten Jahrhundert*, Frankfurt, 1850. (M.P.L. CXXXVIII, 863). Mone thought there were eleven Masses in the set, but Dom A. Wilmart (*Rev. bénéd.* XXVIII, 377 ff.) has convincingly reduced them to seven: six for ordinary Sundays and one for St. Germanus. W. J. Anderson, in *Jour. Theol. Studies*, XXIX (1928), p. 337, has printed fragments of an eighth-century Sacramentary.

problem. The Spanish rite had been officially superseded by the Roman towards the end of the eleventh
century, with the exception of six ancient parish
churches of Toledo, where it struggled for survival
for another two centuries at least; but it was virtually
extinct when the great Cardinal Ximenes de Cisneros
(d. 1517), 'priscarum ceremoniarum studiosissimus
mozarabum,' took measures to revive it. With papal
approbation, he established the Mozarabic Chapel
in his cathedral of Toledo, and for its use published the
Missale Mixtum (in 1500) and the *Breviarium Gothicum*
(in 1502).[1] As source-texts, these must be used with
caution, but modern scholarship has been more for-
tunate in Spain than in France, and has brought to
light a considerable number of important earlier
sources from which the Mozarabic—or, more properly,
Visigothic—liturgy may be studied. The chief of
these, for our purpose, are the *Liber Ordinum* (eleventh
century) and *Liber Mozarabicus Sacramentorum* (ninth
century) edited by Dom M. Férotin—the latter
containing also a more or less detailed précis of several
other liturgical manuscripts—and the *Antiphonarium
Mozarabicum* of León (ninth-tenth century), edited by
the Benedictines of Silos in 1928.[2] In spite of their
comparatively late dates, these documents faithfully
preserve, for the most part, the essential features of
the seventh-century Spanish liturgy.

It would be too much to say that the earlier liturgists
were ever in complete agreement about the Gallican
rite, but until fairly recent times there would have been

[1] See Bibliography.   [2] For all these, see Bibliography.

few dissentients to the general opinion that (*a*) the 'custom of masses' witnessed by Augustine at Arles was the rite described by Germanus; that (*b*) it was the rite in use at that date throughout France; that (*c*) it was fundamentally different from that of Rome; and that (*d*) it had come originally from the East. Some scholars held that it had reached Gaul along with the first missionaries; others that it was the liturgy of Ephesus and St. John, imported by Irenaeus in the second century; still others that it came with the Arian invaders and supplanted the Roman rite. There was virtual agreement that the Gallican and Spanish rites were identical in all essentials, and that Spain derived from Gaul—although some would admit the possibility of African influence in Spain.[1]

Most of these theories, with such modifications as increasing knowledge made necessary, were carried over into modern times. One of them—the Ephesine origin of the Gallican rite—became the favourite thesis of nineteenth-century Anglican liturgists.[2] The really insuperable objection to this, as Duchesne pointed out, is that no rite of the second century could be so elaborate and so dependent upon the calendar as the Gallican rite was, even if it were proper to

[1] One must allow for national sentiment. Most of the early liturgists were French, and Spaniards resented their theories. Even A. Lesley, the Scottish Jesuit, in his edition of the Spanish *Missale mixtum*, is careful to show that even if the two rites were identical and the Gallican earlier, Spain need not have borrowed from Gaul. If the Church of Ephesus sent Irenaeus to Gaul with the Liturgy of St. John in his luggage, why may it not have sent someone else to Spain with another copy?

[2] E.g. J. M. Neale and G. H. Forbes, *The Ancient Liturgies of the Gallican Church* (Burntisland, 1855); F. E. Warren, *The Liturgy and Ritual of the Celtic Church* (Oxford, 1881).

speak of distinct 'rites' at all at that date. Duchesne himself would derive the Gallican use from a form of the Antiochene liturgy brought to Milan in the fourth century, probably by the Arian Bishop Auxentius (d. 374), a native of Cappadocia.[1] The implication here that the Ambrosian rite was originally Gallican, which Duchesne stubbornly defended against all criticism, has become increasingly doubtful, and collapses altogether if (as now seems certain) the treatise *De Sacramentis*, with its Roman canon, is the work of Ambrose himself.[2]

Opposition to Duchesne's thesis came not only from the scholars, like Ceriani and Magistretti, who were specialists on the Ambrosian liturgy, but from others who were working out a new and revolutionary answer to the whole question—viz. that the Gallican rite was nothing in the world but the original Roman rite before that was modified. Probst had perhaps been the first to suggest this, and to attribute drastic changes in the Roman rite to Pope Damasus.[3] But it was Dom Cagin, and after him Dom Cabrol, who made the theory presentable and, up to a point,

---

[1] Duchesne, *Origines du culte chrétien*, 5th ed., Paris, 1925, pp. 95 ff.

[2] G. Morin, in *Jahrbuch für Liturgiewissenschaft* (Maria Laach), VIII (1929), pp. 86 ff.; cf. *Rev. bénéd.* LI (1939), pp. 101 ff. R. H. Connolly, in *Downside Review*, January, 1941; also a privately printed pamphlet: *The* De Sacramentis, *a work of St. Ambrose* (1942). Morin, in 1939, reverted to the view that Milan in the fourth century had a 'Gallican' liturgy, and was the chief centre from which it spread. His argument is difficult to follow, for he attributes the introduction of the rite to the influence of the Arian Goths 'au temps des invasions', and at the same time places it before the accession of Auxentius in 355; Ambrose himself introduced the Roman canon of *De Sacramentis*.

[3] F. Probst, *Liturgie des vierten Jahrhunderts* (Münster i.W., 1893); *Die abendländische Messe von fünften bis zum achten Jahrhundert* (Münster i.W., 1896), pp. 264 ff.

respectable.[1] Its basis is the contrast between the 'uniform euchology' of the Eastern rites and the 'variable euchology' of the Western, both Roman and Gallican. This contrast has perhaps been over-stressed; it would be truer to say that East and West developed different sorts of variability. But a valid distinction remains. Variation in the West is not only, as also in the East, controlled by the Church calendar, but the text of the variable prayers is normally based upon it. When and how this practice arose is uncertain. Probst, not very convincingly, attributed it to Damasus; more probably it began in Gaul, somewhere about 450.[2] Rome, about the same time, adopted the variable Collect of the Day, and the variable Preface, introducing the *Sanctus*. But neither in Gaul nor at Rome are these variable elements the remains of an earlier common use. At most, they witness to a similar conception of the liturgy in its relation to the calendar, and Rome never admitted real variability, as Spain and Gaul did, into the central eucharistic prayer. Anyhow, a 'variable euchology' is not in itself decisive; any regional liturgy might, theoretically, vary its component parts *ad libitum* and still remain quite distinct from other liturgies. Cagin and Cabrol are themselves constrained to explain away, not very successfully, the apparent structural differences between the Western rites.

One other theory remains to be noticed—that of

[1] P. Cagin, in *Paléographie musicale*, V (1896); also *L'Eucharistia*, Paris, 1912. F. Cabrol, *Origines Liturgiques* (Paris, 1906).
[2] See below, p. 46 f.

J. B. Thibaut, put forward in 1929.[1] This has not won nor, I think, deserved any notable measure of acceptance; it involves too many hasty judgements and begged questions, and not a few downright inaccuracies. But it has, nevertheless, some interesting features. Thibaut rightly holds that up till the fifth century the Gallican Mass was substantially the same as the Roman. Then, he thinks, Cassian brought to the West various usages from Jerusalem and Ephesus, which spread from his monastery in Marseilles to Lérins, thence to Arles, and thence (in the sixth century) throughout Gaul, into Britain, and into Spain, where they amalgamated with a rite originally derived from Africa. The theory as a whole is not convincing, but it was worth while to indicate the importance of Arles and of its great bishop, Caesarius, in the Gallican liturgical tradition.

All these theories assume the authenticity of the letters attributed to Germanus, and to a great extent depend upon it. But doubts on this score, tentatively expressed by Koch[2] as long ago as 1900, and more forcibly by O. Bardenhewer and E. Bishop,[3] have now come to a head, and Dom A. Wilmart has made it impossible any longer to ascribe the letters either to Germanus or to his epoch. They are, Wilmart suggests, 'an edifying commentary on the decisions of a Frankish council, otherwise unknown, which

[1] J. B. Thibaut, L'ancienne liturgie gallicane (Paris, 1929). Reviewed by F. Cabrol in Rév. d'hist. ecclés. XXVI (1930), pp. 951 ff.
[2] H. Koch in Theologische Quartalschrift, LXXXII (1900), pp. 528 f.
[3] E. Bishop, Liturgica historica (1918), p. 131—giving 650 as the earliest date to which they can be assigned.

met at the end of the seventh century, or even a little later.' They show strong Spanish influence, and some passages are obviously based upon the *De Ecclesiasticis Officiis* of Isidor (d. 636); but their origin is Gallican and probably Burgundian. They represent, on the whole, a Gallican rite—not *the* Gallican rite, in its pure form (whatever that may have been), but the particular rite of a particular church, at a period of liturgical decadence; possibly the church of Autun, which possesses the unique ninth-century manuscript.[1] Alternatively, they may be, as Séjourné suggests, a 'mystical explanation' of the Mozarabic rite—'one of those adaptations of a foreign liturgical document which were at that time so numerous in Gaul.'[2] Certain, as we shall see, they embody some features which are not Spanish, and are therefore presumably Gallican—or Burgundian.

The collapse of 'Germanus' has indeed altered the whole situation. On the one hand, it simplifies the problem, since it is no longer necessary to find early sources for Eastern borrowings. On the other hand, it makes a confident reconstruction of the earlier Gallican liturgy more difficult than ever. We are thrown back on (1) the very meagre evidence of Gallican councils and writers, such as Caesarius of Arles and Gregory of Tours; (2) the Masses of Mone and such genuine Gallican elements as are embedded in the *Missale Gothicum* and other romanized documents; and (3) whatever equivalence we may

[1] A. Wilmart, article *Germain de Paris (Lettres attribuées à saint)*, in F. Cabrol, *Dict. d'archéol. chrét. et de liturgie*, VI, 1049 (1924).
[2] P. Séjourné, *Saint Isidore de Séville* (Paris, 1929), p. 200.

postulate between the early rites of Gaul and Spain. There is no outside evidence at all, unless we assume— as, it must be admitted, most liturgists have assumed without question—that the letter of Pope Innocent I to Decentius of Gubbio, written in 416, refers to Gallican practices in that Italian diocese, just over 100 miles north of Rome.[1] Now that the Ambrosian rite can no longer be reckoned as Gallican, this does not, on the face of it, seem very likely; and the Pope's letter admits, I think, of a different interpretation. He begins by asserting that all the churches of the West, since they were all founded either by St. Peter or by his successors the Bishops of Rome, ought in all things to follow the usages of Rome, and neither add nor substitute anything which wants authority or seems to imitate some foreign example, 'lest in their zeal for outlandish and independent ways[2] they appear to disregard the source from which they sprang.' On that ground he reprehends two eucharistic practices. 'You tell me that some persons order the (Kiss of) Peace to be given to the people or exchanged among the priests before the consecration of the mysteries, whereas it should, of course, be announced after all those things which I am not permitted to quote'— i.e. the consecration prayer. And then: 'In regard to the recital of the names before the priest makes his prayers (*preces*) and by his praying (*oratione*) commends the offerings of those whose names are to be read out, it is useless—as you, with your usual good sense, will

[1] M.P.L. LXXXIV, 639.
[2] 'peregrinis assertionibus.' *Assertio* was the technical term for the declaration of a slave's freedom.

recognize—to insert a person's name when you have not yet offered his oblation to God, albeit to Him nothing of course is unknown. The oblations, therefore, are to be commended first, and then the names of those whose offerings they are should be read out, so that this naming may come in the course of the sacred mysteries (*inter sacra mysteria*), and not among those other things which are preliminary.'

The order of Innocent's remarks may imply that at Gubbio the Pax preceded the Naming, whereas in the Gallican and Spanish rites the order was reversed;[1] but anyhow, in the Roman rite itself, the Pax had always stood at the beginning of the *Missa fidelium* until Innocent himself, or some one else not long before, had postponed it. Gubbio here simply continued the older custom. The question of the Naming is not so simple. It is quite possible and even probable that Rome also originally recited the names of the offerers at the offertory, and that after their transference into the Canon, their old place was filled by a proper offertory-prayer, the Secret. In any case, Innocent tells Decentius to follow Roman practice, not because it is ancient, but simply because it is Roman; nor does he allege that the customs of Gubbio are novelties, or that they have been directly borrowed from outside. His point is that, since Rome has made changes, persistence in earlier practices will give the impression of disloyalty and cause scandal.[2]

[1] I.e. in all the available evidence. But in Innocent's time the primitive order may have persisted, as at Gubbio.

[2] 'caput institutionum *videantur* omittere.' Cf. the previous phrase: 'aliquid quod . . . aliunde accipere *videatur* exemplum.'

II

PRELIMINARIES

In attempting to reconstruct the Gallican rite of the sixth and seventh centuries, when it reached its fullest development and dispersion, we most presuppose, up to the end of the fourth century, throughout the West—and, indeed, throughout Christendom—one simple and fairly uniform eucharistic rite, made up of the primitive synaxis and the primitive eucharist, more or less neatly welded together into one continuous service. The first half would everywhere consist of a greeting ('The Lord be with you,' etc.), a series of scriptural lections interspersed with psalm-singing, a sermon, the dismissal of non-communicants, and the intercessory prayers of the faithful. The second half would likewise begin with a greeting, and go on with the kiss of peace, the offering of the bread and wine, the great eucharistic prayer, the breaking of the host, and the Communion of the people. After the fourth century, as the result of the break-up of the Empire and the isolation, in varying degrees, of local churches, liturgical differences develop. In some places some of the primitive elements are dropped or shifted; everywhere new and diverse additions are made according to local taste or fashion; there are constant piece-meal borrowings and imitations. The process may be likened to the development of church architecture. The primitive buildings, of simple design and more or less alike, undergo various kinds of reconstruction. A porch is added to one, an aisle to another, a tower to a third; roofs are raised, chancels lengthened, chapels thrown out—not to mention redecorations and refittings. The old fabric, or part of it, remains, but it is not always easily discernible under the mass of later accretions. If we may take the analogy a step further and liken the *Missa fidelium* to the chancel, and the *Missa catechumenorum* to the nave, we find that everywhere, in the fourth and fifth centuries, something in the nature of a porch or narthex has been built on—i.e. an introductory section designed to lead up to the original structure. This was an Eastern innovation, taking different forms in different churches. Rome followed suit, adopting first the Byzantine Entrance-Chant (Introit), and subsequently the Alexandrian Collect (after the greeting), the Antiochene Liturgy (after the Introit), and the Byzantine Hymn (between the Litany and the Greeting)— using for this last not the Greek Trisagion, but the *Gloria in Excelsis*. How Gaul began, or when, it is difficult to say. In 'Germanus' an Entrance-Chant (*Antiphona ad prelegendum*) is followed by the deacon's call for silence and the priest's greeting: 'Dominus sit semper vobiscum,'[1] to which the people reply: 'Et cum spiritu tuo.' Then comes the Trisagion, in Greek and Latin, *Kyrie eleison*, and the canticle *Benedictus*, called (as in other Gallican sources) the *Prophetia*. Of these, the Entrance-Chant is almost certainly an importation from Spain, which had probably got it from Rome in the sixth century; there is no reference to it

[1] This is the invariable Spanish formula.

in any other Gallican source.[1] The Greeting is, of course, primitive, and 'Germanus' preserves a trace of its original function as an introduction to the lections, saying that 'the deacon proclaims silence . . . that by being silent the people may better hear the Word of God.' The Trisagion was also an importation, probably straight from the East and at no very early date. It was certainly not used in Gaul in the early sixth century, since Avitus of Vienne (d. 518), writing to the Burgundian King Gondebaud, praises it as a custom of the 'nobler cities' of the East.[2] Duchesne thinks that it was introduced by the Second Council of Vaison in 529, which rules that 'in all Masses, both early in the morning and in Lent (i.e. after None), as also in those celebrated in commemoration of the departed, *Sanctus, sanctus, sanctus* should always be said just as at public Masses.'[3] But this undoubtedly refers, not to the Trisagion, but to the Latin *Sanctus* after the 'Preface,' which some priests omitted in Lent and at Requiems—or perhaps whenever there was no choir to sing it.[4] There is no good reason to suppose that the Greek Trisagion (or 'Aius') had any place in the Gallican Mass before the seventh century. Apart from 'Germanus,' there is only one other possible reference to its use in Gaul at all—in the Life of St. Gaugericus, a seventh-century

---

[1] The passage in Gregory of Tours, *De gloria martyrum*, I, xxxiv (M.P.L. LXXI, 736), is nothing to the point, *pace* Duchesne.
[2] Avitus, *Epist. iii* (M.P.L. LIX, 210).
[3] Can. iii (M.P.L. LXXXIV, 262).
[4] If the council had meant the *Trisagion*, it would not, in one and the same canon, have dealt first with the *Kyrie* and then with this, for the *Trisagion* always came first.

bishop of Cambrai; and there its liturgical use is only implied.[1] That it subsequently became normal in Gaul and thence got into the Roman Good Friday liturgy, as E. Bishop conjectures, is very probable.[2] It was regularly used in Spain, in the seventh century, on greater festivals.

The Second Council of Vaison—a synod of seventeen Provençal bishops under the presidency of Caesarius of Arles—certainly introduced, or intended to introduce, *Kyries* into the Gallican use, in emulation of 'the Apostolic See and all the provinces of the East and of Italy,' where, it says, the 'pleasant and very helpful custom' has been adopted of saying *Kyrie eleison* 'frequentius.' And the synod prescribes its use 'in all our churches' at Matins, at Mass, and at Vespers.[3] This is, however, not so simple as it looks. It might mean: 'Rome and the rest now use *Kyrie eleison* more frequently (than they did—or, than we do), and therefore we will have it at all the public services'—an interpretation which neither affirms nor denies its previous use at Mass or at the Office. Aurelian of Arles, the successor of Caesarius, in his *Regula ad monachos* (*c.* 547) indeed inserts a threefold *Kyrie* at three points in every office.[4] But there is no

---

[1] *Analecta Bollandiana*, VII (1888), p. 387. (I owe this reference to Dom Gregory Dix, O.S.B.) But is this the *Trisagion* at all? The good bishop, in the course of a 'Rogation,' intones: 'aius, aius, aius per trinum numerum.' This suggests rather a Greek version of the *Sanctus*, such as is found in Spain (*Antiph. León*, p. 291), or the other Spanish form which follows the *Oratio missae*: 'Agios, agios, agios, Domine Deus, rex aeterne, tibi laudes et gratias.'

[2] *Liturgica historica*, pp. 131–3.

[3] Can. iii (M.P.L. LXXXIV, 261).

[4] M.P.L. LXVIII, 394. It does not figure in the Rule of Caesarius, nor in the public offices of the Spanish rite. Cf. E. Bishop, *op. cit.*, p. 126.

evidence of its adoption at Mass, except its presence
in 'Germanus,' and that is not very conclusive.
The single *Kyrie* there, sung by three choir-boys in
unison, is somewhat unimpressive as a following of
the august precedents alleged at Vaison, and anyhow looks less like a distinct liturgical unit than like
an appendage to the Trisagion, which is itself described
as coming 'ante prophetiam.'[1] I am inclined to think
that Vaison produced no results outside its own province, and that 'Germanus' took his Kyrie along with
the Trisagion directly or indirectly from the East.[2]

With the *Benedictus* or *Prophetia* we are on firmer
ground. It is perhaps the one distinctly Gallican
element in this introductory section, and Gregory of
Tours refers to it as the first point in the Mass at
which the celebrant's voice was heard[3]—which seems
to preclude the preliminary Greeting found in
'Germanus.' The latter says that the *Prophetia* was
sung 'alternis vocibus' and (in his second letter[4]) that
it was omitted in Lent. In the liturgical texts it is
sometimes followed by a *Collectio post prophetiam*, and
the presence of this in the seventh-century Masses of

---

[1] 'Aius vero *ante prophetiam* . . . cantatur.'
[2] The only Eastern rite known to have a *Kyrie* after the *Trisagion* is the
Syriac St. James, and it is noteworthy that the greeting in 'Germanus' comes
in the Antiochene place, unlike that of any other Western rite. Gregory of
Tours mentions the *Kyrie* only as part of the Rogation-tide Litany; *Hist. franc.*
X, i (M.P.L. LXXI, 529).
[3] *Hist. franc.* VIII, vii (M.P.L. LXXI, 453). Thibaut's theory (*op. cit.*,
pp. 29 ff.), that it commemorates the baptism of Clovis, is typically adven-
turous.
[4] M.P.L. LXXII, 95: 'Sanctus Deus archangelorum in quadragesimo
concinetur et non canticum Zachariae.' Thibaut jumps to the conclusion
that there was a special Lenten canticle, otherwise unknown, beginning:
'Sanctus Deus archangelorum.' It is, of course, the *Trisagion*, the '*Ἅγιος ὁ
θεός*' of the archangels.

Mone, which are purely Gallican, argues for a fairly early date and against imitation of the Roman Collect of the Day. May it not rather be an extension of the Gallican practice of putting a prayer after the psalmody of the Office? Aetheria noticed this custom in Jerusalem at the end of the fourth century;[1] Cassian attests it 'per omnem orientem,' as well as in his own monastery at Marseilles;[2] the Council of Agde (506) orders it for the public Office;[3] and Caesarius, who presided at Agde, alludes to it in his sermons.[4] The Gallican Collect is primarily based upon the canticle, although allusions to the liturgical occasion are, in the later texts, worked into it, and although it gives place eventually to a Collect of the Day of the Roman kind.[5] It is perhaps the earliest variable element in the Gallican Mass.

III

THE *SYNAXIS*, OR *MISSA CATECHUMENORUM*

The Spanish rite never altered the primitive place of the celebrant's greeting at the beginning of the 'synaxis,' immediately before the first lection, and this may well have been its general position in the Gallican rite. It marks the transition from the 'porch' to the 'nave' of the liturgy.

[1] *Peregrinatio*, XXIV, i (C.S.E.L. XXXIX, 71).
[2] *Institutiones*, II, v (C.S.E.L. XVII, p. 22).
[3] Canon xxx (M.P.L. LXXXIV, 267).
[4] *Sermo lxxvi* (ed. Morin, p. 302).
[5] Spain used the *Gloria* in place of the Gallican *Benedictus*, and an *Oratio post Gloriam* which, as often as not, refers only to the canticle. When it is 'of the day,' it is generally borrowed from the Office, and based upon the preceding antiphon there.

Gaul and Spain had three lections—but there is no need to see in this, as some have, a Gallican characteristic; all Western rites probably had three until the fifth century.[1] The first was normally from the Old Testament, but in Eastertide it might be from the Apocalypse,[2] or on the feast of a martyr from his *Passio*.[3] The second came from the Epistles or the Acts of the Apostles—it was generally called 'the Apostle'—and the third, of course, from the Gospels, often in the form of a cento or 'harmony.'

After the Epistle, 'Germanus' places the *Benedictiones*—i.e. the Song of the Three Children. So does the Lectionary of Luxeuil on one of the two occasions (Low Sunday) when it directs its use; but on the other, Christmas Day, it puts 'Danihel cum benedictione' after the Old Testament lection, which is its regular Spanish position, as ordered by the Fourth Council of Toledo (633) 'in omnium missarum sollemnitate.'[4] And this accords much better with the most

[1] Thibaut attempts to prove that Spain, following what he supposes to be Roman and African precedent, dropped the O.T. lection at a very early date, and resumed it later in imitation of Gaul (*op. cit.*, p. 79). His prooftext, canon iv of the First Council of Toledo (400), does not, however (as Thibaut says), deprive an erring subdeacon 'of his functions as reader'; it says that he is to be reckoned among the doorkeepers or among the readers, 'ita ut evangelium et apostolum non legat'—implying that he could still read the Prophecy. *Cf.* can. ii of the same Council (M.P.L. LXXXIV, 329).
[2] Cf. Lectionary of Luxeuil (M.P.L. LXXII, 199 ff.); Fourth Council of Toledo, can. xvii (M.P.L. LXXXIV, 372).
[3] Caesarius, *Sermones* (ed. Morin, pp. 294, 309); Gregory of Tours, *De mirac. sci. Martini*, II, 29, 79; *De gloria martyrum*, I, 80; Lect. Luxeuil, *passim* (M.P.L. LXXII, 171 ff.); Hilduinus, Letter to Louis the Pious (M.G.H., *Epist. Caroli aevi*. III, p. 330).
[4] Can. xiv (M.P.L. LXXXIV, 371). This regularized, but did not introduce the Canticle, since it complains that some priests leave it out on Sundays and saints' days. It is found on thirteen occasions in the León Antiphoner, in a great variety of versions—some of them attributed to particular authors, such as Isidor and Ildefonse. The Missal of Ximenes calls it 'Tractus,' doubtless because of its position in the Roman Mass of Ember Saturday.

probable explanation of its introduction into the festal Mass—i.e. its position in the liturgy of Holy Saturday, as the conclusion (invariably sung) of the lection from Daniel (iii. 1–24), which in both Spain and Gaul was the last of the Vigil Prophecies, followed by the Epistle of the Mass. Caesarius alludes to it as in regular use: 'You have heard in the *Benedictiones*, and you do hear on every feast-day when they are said, how all things celestial and terrestrial praise God.'[1]

What happened at this point on ordinary days is not easy to determine. Spain always had a *Psallendum* or *Psalmus pulpitalis*. (The *Threnos*, from the Lamentations, which took its place on some Lenten ferias, and the strophic *Preces* which follow it on Lenten Sundays in the modern Missal, are probably not older than the seventh century.[2]) So far as I know, there is no Gallican evidence at all. Psalmody was certainly used in this part of the Mass, for Caesarius can preach from a psalm-text which his people have just heard,[3] but that may refer equally well to a chant between the Epistle and the Gospel. As we have seen, 'Germanus' places the *Benedictiones* there, and he follows it with a *responsorium* sung by the choir-boys. In all probability this is the *psalmus responsorius* known to Gregory of Tours, although he says it was sung by a deacon— he does not say when.[4] In this place it would, of

---

[1] *Sermo lxix* (ed. Morin, p. 278). The prayer 'post benedictionem' in the Bobbio Missal has no connection with this; it is a thanksgiving after Mass.

[2] The *Threnos* appears on eleven days in the León Antiphoner, as against ten in the Missal (where it is called *Tractus*). The *Preces* appear only once in the Antiphoner, on Maundy Thursday, *before* the *Psallendum* (p. 118); but they are said by a deacon, not (as in the Missal) by the priest.

[3] *Sermo cciv* (ed. Morin, p. 776).   [4] *Hist. franc.* VIII, iii.

course, correspond to the Roman *Graduale* and the Ambrosian *Versus in alleluia*, but to nothing in the Spanish rite, where the Gospel followed immediately after the Epistle.[1]

All liturgies began in very early times to surround the liturgical Gospel with honorific ceremonial. The earliest Gallican witness to this is Gregory of Tours, who mentions the procession of the deacon, carrying the 'holy book of the Gospels,' and the people's response to his announcement of it: 'Gloria Deo omnipotenti.'[2] By the time of 'Germanus' there are elaborations. The procession of the Gospel Book—itself covered with a red veil[3]—carries seven lights and is accompanied on its way to the 'tribunal analogii' by the Trisagion in Greek, and by the same in Latin on its return to the sanctuary, both versions being sung by a clerical soloist. When the Gospel is announced, the clerics respond: 'Gloria tibi, Domine.' This, the Roman response, is also found (but said by all the congregation) in the Spanish Beatus of Liébana (ninth century);[4] other Spanish sources have 'Deo gratias' or the simple 'Amen' of the Benedictine Rule.[5] Isidor knows the solemn procession; he defines

---

[1] It is sometimes asserted that the Fourth Council of Toledo shifted the *Laudes* (or *Alleluia*) from before to after the Gospel. But Isidor distinctly says that it came after the Gospel: 'post lectionum praedicationem' (*De eccl. off.* I, xiii), and the Council is plainly correcting the irregularity of those who put it forward. African precedent for the Spanish custom is alleged, but the evidence is far from clear.

[2] *Hist. franc.* VIII, iv. The incident recorded belongs about 571.

[3] *Epist.* ii (M.P.L. LXXII, 96).

[4] M.P.L. XCVI, 935.

[5] *Liber comicus* (ed. Morin), *passim*; but on Good Friday: 'Non respondidatur Deo gratias.' *Liber mozarabicus sacramentorum* (ed. Férotin), 903: 'post evangelium respondeant omnes Amen.' Cf. *Regula Bened.* cap. xi.

acolytes as 'ceroferarii' from their carrying candles when the Gospel is to be read or the sacrifice offered.[1]

Gaul—or at least Provence—seems to have been unusually conservative in retaining the sermon after the Gospel, which elsewhere tended to drop out of normal use. Caesarius is very emphatic that not only bishops in their cathedrals, but also priests and deacons in parish churches could and should preach frequently;[2] and the Council of Vaison is probably following his lead in its second canon, which gives authority to parish priests to preach their own sermons (*verbum faciendi*) and orders deacons, when no priest is present, to read a homily from the Fathers.[3] Spain provided books of sermons, such as the Homiliary of Toledo, for the same purpose.

After the sermon, in the primitive rite, came the dismissal of catechumens and penitents, and then the Prayers of the Faithful, in some such form as that of the Great Intercessions in the Roman Good Friday liturgy, brought the synaxis to a definite close. But no church in Christendom kept strictly to the original scheme, and no part of the liturgical fabric has undergone such varied and repeated reconstruction as this junction of 'nave' and 'chancel.' Rome, by the sixth century, had dropped the dismissals altogether,[4] and

---

[1] *De eccl. off.* II, xiv. The Antiphoner of León (p. 123) directs that on Good Friday lights and cross be not carried, and the book not covered.

[2] *Sermo i* (ed. Morin, p. 11). Gregory of Tours has no reference to a sermon at Mass.

[3] Can. ii (M.P.L. LXXXIV, 261).

[4] [But St. Gregory the Great refers to the deacon's customary (*ex more*) dismissal of persons not qualified to communicate, 'si quis non communicat, det locum': see *Dialogues* II, 23, ed. U. Moricca, Fonti per la Storia d'Italia, Rome 1924, p. 115.—E.C.R.]

reduced the Prayers of the Faithful to one word: 'Oremus'—if indeed that does not represent an entirely different prayer. Spain and Gaul kept the dismissals, but before them 'Germanus' inserts a prayer 'pro populo,' in which 'the deacons pray for the people, and the priests, prostrate before the Lord, intercede for the people's sins.' Duchesne calls this the beginning of the Prayers of the Faithful,[1] but that is misleading; it is evidently a diaconal litany of the Eastern type, such as became fashionable in the West after the old Prayers of the Faithful had begun to drop out of use. At one time or another it found a place in every Western liturgy, except the African. Pope Gelasius, about 495, put it after the Introit, where it remained in the Roman rite on some days down to the ninth century, although Gregory the Great replaced it on 'ordinary days' by the ninefold *Kyrie*. Milan still has it, at the same point, on Sundays in Lent. The Spanish evidence is obscure; the curious strophic *Preces* after the Old Testament lection on Lenten Sundays in the modern Missal are probably not very ancient, though they may have superseded earlier litanies of the usual type,[2] and these may be what Isidor means by the *preces* 'against the sicknesses of the soul' which he says were first composed by the Greeks.[3] The position of the litany in the Stowe Missal between the Epistle and Gospel—there being no Old Testament lection—may derive from this, in spite of its attribution to St. Martin, Or, of course, 'Germanus' may not represent the general Gallican

[1] *Origines*, p. 208.   [2] See above, p. 26, note 2.   [3] *De eccl. off.* I, viii.

practice; the only other evidence is the *Collectio post precem* which appears on two days only (Christmas and Easter) in the *Missale Gothicum*, between the *Collectio post prophetiam* and the *Praefatio*,—and that is only conclusive as against the Gelasian position. It is noteworthy that 'Germanus' alone explicitly places his litany at a point exactly corresponding to the Byzantine *Ektene*, before the Dismissals; it may well be another of his direct Eastern borrowings.

As we have said, Spain and Gaul retained the Dismissals.[1] A rubric in the León Antiphoner gives what looks like a fairly primitive form. The deacon says: 'Competentes orate. Humiliate vos ante Dominum. Completa oratione vestra, simul Deo gratias agentes, dicite Amen.' They respond: 'Amen.' Again the deacon says: 'Accedite ad signaculum, et ite cum pace.' They all say: 'Deo gratias.'[2] In the East the deacon led the prayers of those about to be dismissed, in the form of a litany, to which they responded 'Kyrie eleison,' and which was followed by a prayer of the celebrant; and this is plainly what 'Germanus' means when he says that the deacons pray for the catechumens, the priest says a collect 'post precem,' and they go out.

Here should follow the proper Prayers of the Faithful, and there is good evidence that Gaul did indeed retain them considerably longer than Rome. The

[1] Council of Epaon (517), can. xxix; of Valentia (524), can. i; of Lérida (546), can. iv. Cf. Isidor, *Etymol.* VI, xix. 4: 'clamante levita, si quis catechumenus remansit, exeat foris.'
[2] Antiph. León, p. 90. Cf. the dismissal of penitents in the Missal (M.P.L. LXXXV, 307), and its prototype in *Cod. tolet.* 35. 5 (*Lib. moz. sacr.*, 723).

allusion of Caesarius to the deacon's 'Flectamus genua'[1] seems to refer to these rather than to a diaconal litany, and so does the canon of Lyons (c. 517) which permits penitents to remain in church 'usque ad orationem plebis quae post evangelia legeretur.'[2] What happened after that? Did they simply drop out and leave no trace behind? In 'Germanus,' indeed, the Dismissal is followed at once by the *Sonum*, the chant which accompanies the solemn Procession of the Oblations. So, too, in the Spanish books, where the chant is called the *Sacrificium*, and where it is followed by the *Missa* and *Alia*, which Isidor describes as the first two prayers of the Mass—corresponding to the Gallican *Praefatio* and *Collectio*. These two formulas—which 'Germanus' does not mention at all—present what is perhaps the most puzzling feature of the whole rite. Do they belong where we find them, after the Offertory, as a Gallican form of the Milanese *Oratio super sindonem*, with a long and didactic introduction? That is, naturally, Duchesne's theory.[3] Or do they properly belong before the Offertory, as a development of the introductory and concluding formulas of the Prayers of the Faithful, as Séjourné and others think?[4] With some diffidence I incline to the latter view. In the first place, it accords well with Isidor's description of the two prayers: of the first as 'a prayer of admonition addressed to the people, that

[1] *Sermo lxxvii* (ed. Morin, p. 305).
[2] Mansi, VIII, p. 567.   [3] *Origines*, p. 218.
[4] *Op. cit.*, pp. 174 ff. This is implied in W. C. Bishop, *The Mozarabic and Ambrosian Rites* (London, 1924), p. 31—although he does not notice their anomalous position.

they be stirred up to pray earnestly unto God'; and
of the second as an 'invocation to God, that He will
mercifully accept the prayers of the faithful (*preces
fidelium*) and their oblations.'[1] Secondly, it explains—
as the other theory does not—that which comes
between the two prayers in the Spanish rite. Doubtless
there was at first an interval of silence, later filled
by the singing of 'Hagios, hagios, hagios, Domine
Deus, Rex aeterne, tibi laudes et gratias.'[2] Then the
priest—*not* the deacon—bids: 'Let us remember (*in
mente habeamus*) in our prayers the Holy Catholic
Church, that the Lord may mercifully vouchsafe to
increase it in faith, hope, and love. . . . Let us remember all the lapsed, the captive, the sick, and the exiled
(*peregrinos*), that the Lord may vouchsafe to look
favourably upon them, to redeem them, heal them,
and comfort them.'[3] The people respond: 'Grant this,
eternal almighty God.' The deacon says: 'Stand up'—
implying an earlier command to kneel, which has
dropped out—and the priest says the *Alia*. All this
certainly looks like an abbreviated version of the old
Prayers. There would be no difficulty if it did not
come, in all the extant sources,[4] after the Great
Entrance, and if the two prayers themselves did not
almost invariably appear as long variable formulas

[1] *De eccl. off.* I, xv (M.P.L. LXXXIII, 752)—written about 600.
[2] See above, p. 22, note 1.
[3] This is from the Missal (M.P.L. LXXXV, 540). For another form, see
Liber ordinum, 234. The phrase 'in mente habeamus' is certainly archaic, and
it has often been remarked that a prayer of this sort seems to underlie the
words of Fructuosus, bishop and martyr of Tarragona, A.D. 259: 'In mente
me habere necesse est ecclesiam catholicam, ab Oriente usque in Occidentem
diffusam' (Ruinart, *Acta martyrum*, ed. 1859, p. 266).
[4] The Gallican position must be deduced from the title, *Collectio ante
nomina*, given to this prayer in the Masses of Mone.

concerned only with the current season or festival of the calendar. I suggest, not that their position has been altered, but that the Great Entrance, perhaps from the time of its first introduction (*c.* 590), was put before them—probably for quite practical reasons.[1] This would inevitably tend to alter the function and character of these prayers, and there is nothing very surprising in their subsequent development, given the Gothic passion for hagiolatry and long-windedness; other parts of the Mass suffered no less from it. The earlier tradition may still be seen in some of the simpler formulas, such as those of the Masses of Mone for 'quotidian' Sundays.

IV

THE *MISSA FIDELIUM*

At whatever point the Procession of the Oblations took place, it properly belonged to the Mass of the Faithful, as leading up to the Offertory. Traditionally, it should be preceded by the celebrant's Greeting and the Kiss of Peace; but the Greeting is recorded only in the Mozarabic Missal, where it precedes the *Missa*, and the Pax comes at a later point both in 'Germanus'— the only Gallican evidence—and in the Spanish texts. The Procession itself probably reached both Spain and Gaul late in the sixth century, as the latest thing from Byzantium, with which both countries at that time had close relations. Caesarius does not mention

---

[1] There is indeed evidence that in Spain it was sometimes put at an even earlier point, after the sermon and before the dismissals; cf. *Antiph. León*, 90: 'explicito sacrificio, dicit diaconus, Conpetentes orate,' etc.

it, and his sermons refer more than once to the individual offerings brought to church by the laity, as also do the canons of Mâcon (585).[1] But Gregory of Tours knows of it, and adds the detail that the 'mystery of the Lord's body' is borne by a deacon in a 'turris'[2]—which is the same word that 'Germanus' uses. The accompanying chant, according to 'Germanus,' ends (like the Eastern *Cherubicon*) with a threefold *Alleluia*, during which the priest covers the oblations with a silken veil or 'co-opertorium.' Here follow, in all the extant sources, the *Praefatio* and *Collectio*, which we have sufficiently discussed, and after them the 'Names' and the prayer *Post nomina* or proper Offertory Prayer. The recitation of names 'ad altare cum oblatione' is attested by the Spanish Council of Elvira (*c.* 300),[3] and there is no good reason to doubt that this was the general primitive practice, at least in the West, although Rome at an early date (fourth century) moved the Names into the first part of the canon. To speak of these as 'diptychs' is misleading. They were primarily the names of the actual 'offerers' or communicants present at the Mass, along with others for whom their prayers were desired, such as the diocesan bishop, the local clergy, the founders and

---

[1] *Sermones xiii, xiv* (ed. Morin, pp. 63, 69); Council of Mâcon, can. iv (Mansi, IX, 947). Thibaut conjectures that the Procession, with its chant, was the 'new custom of psalmody,' which Caesarius introduced with gratifying success at Arles (*Sermo lxxv,* ed. Morin, p. 300). This is not very likely; whatever the innovation was, Caesarius says that it was already the custom of 'neighbouring cities,' and that he had desired to adopt it for 'many years.'

[2] *Liber miraculorum,* I, 86 (M.P.L. LXXI, 781).

[3] Can. xxix (M.P.L. LXXXIV, 305). Thibaut (*op. cit.,* p. 80) forces this to mean 'in the Canon,' in order to support his thesis that the Gallican practice had no parallel in the West until Spain, at a later date, adopted it.

benefactors of the church,[1] the sick, etc. If the dead
were mentioned at all—and it is hard to believe that
they were not—they, too, were local people ('cari
nostri'). Local or national martyrs, and perhaps others,
might be commemorated on their anniversaries,[2] even
before Jerusalem set the fashion of naming a long list
of scriptural saints and departed bishops at every
Eucharist. These names were apparently recited by
the deacons, with some sort of response sung by the
choir.[3] The formula in the *Liber Ordinum*, apart from
the list of saints with which it begins and which is
obviously an interpolation, may be taken as typical,
though probably abbreviated: 'Our priests of God,
N. the Roman Pope,[4] NN., and the rest, offer the
oblation to the Lord God. Likewise all the presbyters
and the deacons offer, making memorial for themselves
and all the clergy and the whole brotherhood. The
servant of God, N., offers, with his wife and children
and all his dependents (*fidelibus*), that the Lord may
vouchsafe to aid and uphold them in their good works.
All the people offer, that the Lord may hear their
prayers and supplications. The Holy Catholic Church
of God offers for the spirits and souls of all the faithful
departed, that the Lord may mercifully enrol them

---

[1] The Council of Mérida (666), can. xix (M.P.L. LXXXIV, 623), orders
the naming, on Sundays, of founders and benefactors, living or dead, in
any church which has a priest-in-charge.

[2] Walafrid Strabo, *De rebus eccl.* xxviii (M.P.L. CXIV, 962), says that the
Emperor Theodosius publicly commended Gregory of Cordova for reciting
the names of martyrs on their anniversaries.

[3] *Lib. moz. sacr.* 546: 'Nomina . . . quae levitarum et cantorum tuorum
officiis recitata sunt.' *Antiph. León*, 110: 'Quando nomina offeruntur iuxta
consuetudinem a clero responduntur.' Cf. *ibid.* 118–19; *Lib. ord.*, 186.

[4] The Second Council of Vaison, can. iv, orders the inclusion of the Pope's
name (M.P.L. LXXXIV, 262).

among the ranks of the blessed.'[1] The *Post nomina* prayer, as described by Isidor—'pro offerentibus sive pro fidelibus defunctis[2]'—and as exemplified by most of the existing specimens, both Gallican and Spanish, follows naturally upon some such formula as this. But with the disuse of the people's offerings in kind, the names of the local laity would tend to drop out, while imitation of the East would bring in strings of saints and departed notables. This stage is represented by the Gallican 'diptych' of the dead appended to the *Regula monachorum* of Aurelian of Arles,[3] where the list of 'our fathers and founders' is carried down to King Childebert I (d. 558) and his queen Ultrogotha, and that of the saints down to Caesarius, Aurelian's immediate predecessor—but not without the remembrance also of 'all the faithful departed of this place'; and it should be noted, too, that here the saints are named as intercessors, not as objects of veneration. In the diptychs of the Mozarabic Missal—as in the Stowe Missal (eighth century)—the local note has almost entirely disappeared;[4] the oblation is now the Sacrifice itself, not the materials for it, and it is offered by the priest for himself and for the Church, and to commemorate the saints.[5] 'Germanus' mentions only the naming of the dead, with the detail that while it takes place the veil is lifted from the oblations.

[1] *Lib. ord.*, 235.   [2] *De eccl. off.* I, xv (M.P.L. LXXXIII, 753).
[3] M.P.L. LXVIII, 395. The opening words: 'Simulque precantes,' may imply that the names of the living have preceded it.
[4] M.P.L. LXXXV, 541; Stowe Missal (ed. Warner), II, 6. The Mozarabic form is the older, and probably the source of the Celtic. It retains the 'populi circumstantes' among the offerers.
[5] A few *Post nomina* prayers seem to imply this commemoration of saints; cf. *Missale Gothicum*, nos. 421, 427 (M.P.L. LXXII, 302, 303).

At this point, in both Gaul and Spain, comes the Kiss of Peace, preceded by a variable *Oratio ad pacem*, of which the purpose is, according to Isidor, 'that all who are united together in charity may worthily share in the sacrament of the Body and Blood of Christ.'[1] When or why these rites shifted the Pax from its primitive place before the Offertory and the Naming, it is impossible to say. The Spanish books neatly link it up with the 'Grace' which, in all the Eastern rites, introduces the *Anaphora*; thus, in the *Liber Ordinum*:[2] 'The grace of God the Father almighty, the peace and love of our Lord Jesus Christ, and the fellowship (*societas*) of the Holy Spirit be ever with you all,' with the response: 'And with men of good will'; after which the deacon says: 'Give the peace among yourselves,'[3] and the choir sings the *Antiphona ad pacem*. Of all this our Gallican sources have no trace, unless it be the words in Tyronian notation which appear in the margins of the *Missale Gothicum* opposite *Ad pacem* collects: once, 'Pax et caritas Domini nostri Iesu Christi sit semper vobiscum,' and once, 'Pax, fides, caritas Domini (nostri Iesu) Christi et omnium sanctorum sit semper vobiscum.'[4] In 'Germanus' a similar formula appears later in the rite, as a blessing before Communion.[5]

The Gallican and Spanish anaphoras, although

[1] *De eccl. off.* I, xv (*ut supra*).
[2] *Lib. ord.*, 236. Cf. *Apost. Const.* VIII.
[3] *Antiph. León*, 119. The Missal has: 'Quomodo adstatis, pacem facite.'
[4] Cf. Stowe Missal: 'Pax et caritas Domini nostri Iesu Christi et communicatio omnium sanctorum sit semper vobiscum'—in the Roman position.
[5] See below, p. 44. The phrase, 'pacem Christi'—which Duchesne unwarrantably alters to 'pacem Christiani (proferunt)'—may hint at an earlier tradition.

some of their component parts bore different names, were structurally identical and probably very similar in detail. The Gallican evidence is very scanty for anything except the main variable prayers; even the opening dialogue is nowhere given in full. Caesarius implies that it began with 'Sursum corda' and its response, which he quotes more than once.[1] But to this the Spanish rite, from very early times, prefixed the admonition, probably said by the deacon, 'Aures ad Dominum,' with the same response, 'Habemus ad Dominum nostrum'; and this may have been known in Gaul.[2] Nowhere do we find the preliminary Greeting.

Upon the dialogue follows the *Contestatio* (the Spanish *Illatio*—corresponding to the Roman Preface), different at every Mass and often of great length.[3] This leads up to the *Sanctus* and *Benedictus*. Caesarius clearly implies that these were sung by all the congregation,[4] but he does not quote the full formula, which may or may not have had the peculiarities found in the Spanish texts: 'Sanctus, sanctus, sanctus, Dominus Deus Sabaoth. Pleni sunt caeli et terra gloria maiestatis tuae. Osanna Filio David. Benedictus qui venit in nomine Domini. Osanna in excelsis.'[5]

---

[1] *Sermones xxxiii, xxxiv* (ed. Morin, pp. 97, 141).

[2] It is assigned to the deacon in the treatise *De septem ordinibus ecclesiae* (M.P.L. XXX, 153), which Morin thinks was written in southern Gaul *c.* 417; see *Rév. d'hist. eccl.* XXXIV (1938), p. 237. Cf. Isidor, *Ep. ad Leudefredum* (M.P.L. LXXXIII, 895)—although this is of doubtful authenticity.

[3] The Gallican texts sometimes call it *Immolatio*—probably from a misunderstanding of the Spanish name. *Contestatio* is the word used by Gregory of Tours, *Vita S. Martini*, II, xiv (M.P.L. LXXI, 946).

[4] *Sermo lxiii* (ed. Morin, p. 294). Cf. *Antiph. León*, 119: 'ab omnibus'; *Lib. ord.*, 191: ' a clero.'

[5] The only parallel to 'Osanna Filio David' occurs in the Nestorian Liturgy of Addai and Mari (F. E. Brightman, *Liturgies Eastern and Western*, I, 283).

Both in Gaul and Spain a variable *Post sanctus*, beginning almost always with the words, 'Vere sanctus,'
led up to the narrative of the Institution, or *Missa
secreta*. But at this point there is a notable divergence
between the two rites. The Gallican sources, although
they contain no full text of the formula, invariably
give its *incipit* as 'Qui pridie'—the Roman form;[1]
while Spain, on the contrary, used the Eastern form:
'In qua nocte tradebatur.' But the prayer which
follows, and which in Gaul is named the *Post secreta*
or *Post mysterium*, is in Spain called the *Post pridie*;
and this may imply that the Eastern form is a later
importation.[2] In both liturgies the Sign of the Cross
accompanied or followed the Words of Consecration,[3]
and it is possible that in Gaul, as in Spain, the people
responded: 'Sic credimus, Domine Deus.'[4]

Isidor describes the prayer which follows—i.e.
the *Post pridie* or *Post secreta*—as 'conformatio sacramenti, ut oblatio, quae Deo offertur, sanctificata per
Spiritum, Christi corpori ac sanguini conformetur,'[5]
and it has been vigorously argued (chiefly by Anglican
scholars) that there was originally at this point a
consecratory epiclesis of the Eastern sort, and that
its actual absence from the great majority of the extant

[1] On two occasions, when even this formula admitted variations, the *Missale
gall. vetus* gives a little more of it; M.P.L. LXXII, 345, 347.
[2] There are two variants in *Lib. ord.* (col. 238); but neither is exactly
Scriptural or Eastern. Cf. *Antiph. León*, 117; *Lib. moz. sacr.*, 244.
[3] Gregory of Tours, *Vita patrum*, xvi, 2 (M.P.L. LXXI, 1075).
[4] *Lib. ord.*, 238. A considerable number of *Post pridie* prayers begin with
'Credimus'; also two *Post secreta* prayers in *Missale gothicum*, nos. 19, 516
(M.P.L. LXXII, 228, 314).
[5] *De eccl. off.* I, xv. Some MSS. have 'confirmatio' and 'confirmetur,' and
some scholars, including P. Séjourné and F. Cabrol, accept this reading.

formulas is the result of 'romanization.'[1] There are
solid reasons for rejecting this theory in respect of the
Spanish rite,[2] and I believe they apply equally well
to the Gallican, although the evidence there is much
scantier and Roman influence much more apparent.
The Masses of Mone, which alone show no such
influence, provide six examples.[3] Of these, two have
no hint of any epiclesis, a third prays for the descent
of 'the fulness of thy majesty, divinity, piety, virtue,
and blessing,' two others ask for 'the sprinkling of the
dew of the Holy Spirit' upon the sacrifice; and in all
these last three the object expressed is that it may
become to the communicants 'legitima eucharistia.'[4]
The one formula which goes beyond this is also found
in a Spanish Mass of which the *Illatio* is attributed
to Julian of Toledo (d. 690);[5] it runs (in the better
Spanish text): 'ut his creaturis superpositis altario
tuo Spiritum sanctificationis infundas, ut per trans-
fusionem coelestis atque invisibilis sacramenti, panis
hic transmutatus in carnem, et calix transmutatus in
sanguinem, sit offerentibus gratia et sumentibus
medicina.' Since the Mone Masses belong to the
middle of the seventh century, this cannot be the work
of Julian, though it may well be Spanish; it is quite
obviously not primitive. And in any case it is

[1] Most recently by W. H. Frere, *The Anaphora* (London, 1938), pp. 106,
107.
[2] See my article, 'The Mozarabic Post Pridie,' in *Jour. Theol. Studies*, XLIV
(Oct. 1943), p. 182.
[3] There are nineteen examples in *Miss. Goth.*, three in *Miss. gall. vetus.*
[4] Frere says (*op. cit.*, p. 167) that this phrase betrays 'the hand of the
minimizing Innovator,' and yet recognizes (*ibid.* p. 105, note) that the Mone
Masses are 'the only book not romanized'!
[5] *Lib. moz. sacr.*, 625. The attribution to Julian is in the *Apologia* of Abbot
Samson (d. 890) (Florez, *España sagrada*, XI, 300).

equivocal; the past participle ('transmutatus') may mean *already* changed,' and if so, the formula is in no way exceptional. Wilmart's opinion may be accepted as final: 'The epiclesis of the Gallican and Mozarabic books . . . is quite artificial . . ., the result of a "harmonization" easily explained by Eastern influence in the sixth and seventh centuries.'[1]

The Fraction of the Host followed here, in its primitive place, and in a form which is unprecedented. 'Germanus' does not describe it, but alludes to the fifth-century legend of the Abbot Arsenius, who at the moment of the Fraction saw upon the altar the bleeding body of a child, and an angel who caught its blood in the chalice.[2] There may be some connection between this story and the custom of arranging the fragments of the Host upon the paten in the form of a human body[3]—a custom forbidden by the Second Council of Tours in 567.[4] The council orders the particles to be placed in the form of a cross, and this was doubtless the earlier practice, since we also find it in the Mozarabic books and, with characteristic exaggerations, in the Celtic rite of the tenth and

[1] *Rev. bénéd.* XXVIII (1911), p. 387, note.

[2] The story is in the *Apophthegmata patrum* (M.P.L. LXXIII, 978), translated from the Greek original about 550. Cf. Batiffol, *Études de liturgie*, etc., pp. 288 ff.

[3] Thibaut (*op. cit.*, p. 64) thinks that the legend gave rise to the custom.

[4] Can. iii: 'ut corpus Domini in altari non in imaginario ordine, sed sub crucis titulo componatur.' For other interpretations of this canon see Mabillon in M.P.L. LXXII, 164–6. Duchesne (*op. cit.*, p. 232, note), followed by Thibaut, thinks that this is the practice reprobated by Pope Pelagius I in his letter to Sapaudus of Arles about 558, where he speaks of an 'idolum ex similagine' of which the various members—'ears, eyes, hands,' etc.—are distributed to the faithful 'quasi unicuique pro merito' (M.G.H., *Epist. III*, p. 442). I cannot believe that this has any reference to the eucharistic *Fractio*, but it might mean some sort of *eulogia* or *pain-bénit*, baked in the form of a human body and broken into fragments for distribution after Mass.

eleventh centuries.[1] The Missal of Ximenes prescribes a fraction into nine particles, each with its proper name: 'corporatio, nativitas, circumcisio, apparitio (i.e. Epiphany), passio, mors, resurrectio, gloria, regnum.' But an earlier text, the eleventh-century *Rituale* of Madrid,[2] provides for only seven particles —omitting 'circumcisio' and 'apparitio'—with the explanation: 'Haec sunt septum signacula'. There is here an obvious reference to the Commentary on the Apocalypse of Apringius of Beja (early sixth century), where precisely these names are given to the 'seven seals' of Revelation v. 1—although their application to the eucharistic Fraction may be a later development,[3] and it is quite impossible to say whether or not the same symbolism was ever used in Gaul.

'Germanus' says that the 'supplex clerus' accompanied the Fraction with an antiphon—the *Ad confractionem panis* of the Spanish rite; and after this would come the Lord's Prayer, with its variable preamble and embolism. Spain, in 589, introduced the Nicene Creed after the Fraction,[4] and in later times this led to some dislocation; but the proper order is perfectly explicit in the Antiphoner of León, in the rubric on

[1] Stowe Missal (ed. Warner), II, 41.
[2] *Lib. ord.*, 239, note.
[3] *Apringius de Béja. Son commentaire de l'Apocalypse*, ed. M. Férotin, Paris, 1900, p. 32. The passage reappears in Ildefonsus, *De cognitione baptismi*, xix (M.P.L. XCVI, 120), and in Heterius and Beatus, *Epist. ad Elipandum*, I, cxiii (*ibid.* 964)—in both cases in a vaguely eucharistic context. The nearest parallel—with no eucharistic reference—is Hilary of Poitiers, *Tractatus super Psalmos* (C.S.E.L. XXII, pp. 7–8); I owe this reference to Dom L. Brou, O.S.B.
[4] Third Council of Toledo (589), can. ii (M.P.L. LXXXIV, 351). In the Missal of Ximenes the Fraction is made during the Creed, and the proper antiphon sometimes, but not always, transferred to accompany the *Commixtio* after the *Pater*.

Maundy Thursday: 'After this antiphon (*Ad confractionem*) the Nicene Creed and the Lord's Prayer are recited by all.'[1] In Gaul, too, the whole congregation said the Prayer, as in the East, from very early times.[2] And doubtless there, as in Spain, the *commixtio* followed the priest's embolism, perhaps accompanied by a similar adaptation of an Eastern formula: 'Sancta sanctis, et coniunctio corporis et sanguinis Domini nostri Iesu Christi edentibus et bibentibus sit in vitam aeternam,' with three versicles and 'agios, agios, agios, kyrie o theos.'[3]

V

THE COMMUNION

The blessing of the people in preparation for Communion was normal in all the Western rites—as also in Egypt and the East—up to the end of the fourth century; Gaul and Spain retained it after Rome had dropped it. The Council of Agde (506) restricts it to bishops,[4] but the First Council of Orléans, five years later, allows a priest to bless if the bishop is not

---

[1] *Antiph. León*, 119.

[2] Caesarius, *Sermones xxxv, lxiii* (ed. Morin, pp. 144, 294); Gregory of Tours, *Vita S. Martini*, II, xxx (MPL. LXXI, 955). *Cf.* Cassian, *Collationes* IX, 22 (C.S.E.L. XII, 271).

[3] *Lib. moz. sacr.*, 53, note; 896. *Antiph. León*, lxii. In the *Lib. ordinum* (cols. 241, 322, note)—as in later French sources—the formula has become 'Sancta cum sanctis,' etc., without versicles and said by the priest alone at the *commixtio*. Allusions to the formula in Fastidius (early fifth century), as a *praefatio* before Communion, may well imply its early use in Gaul; see his *Works*, ed. R. S. T. Haslehurst (London, 1927), pp. 103, 218. I owe this reference also to Dom L. Brou, O.S.B., who is preparing a valuable monograph on the Western use of the *Sancta sanctis*. [See his article 'Le "Sancta Sanctis" en Occident,' *Jour. Theol. Studies* XLVI, pp. 160–78; XLVII, pp. 11–29. —E.C.R.]

[4] Canons xliv, xlvii (M.P.L. LXXXIV, 270).

present.[1] Caesarius alludes both to the blessing and to the deacon's preliminary admonition: 'Humiliate vos benedictioni'[2]—to which, in Spain at least, the people responded: 'Deo gratias.' According to 'Germanus' the 'canons lay it down' that, to safeguard the bishop's dignity, he should pronounce a 'longer' blessing, while the priest is to use the shorter form: 'Pax fides et caritas et communicatio corporis et sanguinis Domini sit semper vobiscum.' No such canonical rule is known, nor does this particular form of blessing appear elsewhere, except—word for word, at the same point, and for priests only—in the mediae-val Lyons rite.[3] The Masses of Mone contain no blessings at all; the *Missale Gothicum* and all the Spanish books provide each Mass with its own proper bless-ing, usually in three clauses, but sometimes more, to each of which the people answer 'Amen.'

On ordinary occasions, a large part of the congrega-tion probably departed after the Blessing. Those who remained would be invited by the deacon to take their places for Communion—'Locis vestris accedite' is the Spanish formula, with the response: 'Deo gratias'[4] —and as they did so, the choir would sing the antiphon *Ad accedentes*. 'Germanus' calls this the 'Trecanum,' and expatiates upon it as a symbol of the Trinity—a cryptic passage, of which Thibaut has advanced a somewhat fanciful explanation: i.e. that 'Trecanum'

[1] Can. xxii (M.P.L. LXXXIV, 277). Thibaut (*op. cit.*, p. 71) reads 'fuerit' for 'defuerit,' denying the concession.

[2] Caesarius, *Sermo lxxvi* (ed. Morin, p. 303); cf. *Sermo lxiii* (*ibid.*, p. 294).

[3] D. Buenner, *L'ancienne liturgie romaine—Le rite Lyonnais* (Lyons, 1934), p. 278.

[4] *Lib. ord.*, 241.

represents the Greek τρίκανων and is a name for Psalm xxxiii, of which the Roman number, with its tripled letters, was given a mystical significance.[1] This psalm was indeed, in whole or in part, the normal Eastern Communion-chant;[2] and selected verses from it, with alleluias, form one of the variable chants used at this point in the Spanish rite.[3] But its use in Gaul must remain conjectural, though not improbable; perhaps the strongest evidence for it is the phrase in 'Germanus': 'Jam vero *quam dulcis* sit animae et corporis sacra communio.'[4]

The laity received communion, according to Gregory of Tours, 'ad altarium,' and undoubtedly in both kinds.[5] Men received the host in their bare hands—which Caesarius tells them to wash before they come; but women brought white linen cloths, known as 'dominicales,' with which to cover their hands.[6] The Words of Administration have not been preserved, except in the eleventh-century Spanish *Rituale* of Madrid, where they are: 'Corpus Domini nostri Iesu Christi sit salvatio tua' and 'Sanguis

---

[1] Thibaut, *op. cit.*, pp. 72–4. The identification with the Spanish antiphon, 'Gustate et videte' (from Psalm xxxiii), is accepted by Duchesne (*op. cit.*, p. 238), as previously by P. Lebrun, without question.

[2] *Const. Apost.* VIII; Cyril of Jerusalem, *Mystagog.* v; Liturgy of St. James, etc.

[3] *Lib. ord.*, 241. Cf. *ibid.* 85–6, notes, where other antiphons are provided for Lent and Eastertide. The León Antiphoner has still others.

[4] M.P.L. LXXII, 94. The allusion in Caesarius, *Sermo clxxxvi* (ed. Morin, p. 717), is not conclusive; it appears to refer to a psalm sung before the sermon. But the use of some psalmody at the time of Communion is certain; cf. Aurelian, *Regula* (M.P.L. LXVIII, 396, 406): 'psallendo omnes communicent.'

[5] *Hist. franc.* IX, 3; X, 8. Cf. the Second Council of Tours, can. iv.

[6] Caesarius, *Sermo ccxxvii* (ed. Morin, p. 854). Cf. Council of Auxerre (*c.* 578), canons xxxvi, xlii.

Christi maneat tecum redemptio vera.'[1] Nor is there any trace in Gallican sources of the antiphon after Communion which appears in the Spanish texts.[2] Both rites, however, have prayers after Communion: the Spanish a single collect, called the *Completorium*, and the Gallican a brief exhortation to thankfulness (*Post eucharistiam*), followed by a *Collectio* or *Consummatio missae*.[3] After this the deacon dismissed the people with a formula which has not been preserved, but which was doubtless similar to that of the Spanish *Liber Sacramentorum*: 'Solemnia completa est. In nomine Domini nostri Iesu Christi eamus cum pace.'[4] This was the end of the rite, but there is early evidence for the custom of distributing *eulogiae*, blessed bread (and probably wine), to those who had not communicated.[5]

VI

GENERAL CHARACTERISTICS

The foregoing account will have made clear the one outstanding feature of the Gallican and Spanish rites, viz. their use, even in the central eucharistic prayer, of formulas varying from day to day according to the calendar. This is the Western type of variability and cannot, of course, be more primitive than the

---

[1] *Lib. ord.*, 231, note. Cf. Ildefonse, *De cognitione bapt.* cxxxvii (M.P.L. XCVI, 169): 'Audis ergo Corpus Christi, et respondes Amen.'
[2] *Lib. ord.*, 242, 312; *Antiph. León*, 69.
[3] In *Missale Gothicum* both formulas are sometimes prayers.
[4] The Stowe Missal has simply: 'Missa acta est—In pace.' The Missal of Ximenes expands: 'Solemnia completa sunt in nomine Domini nostri Iesu Christi; votum nostrum sit acceptum cum pace. ℞. Deo gratias.'
[5] Gregory of Tours, *Hist. franc.* V, xiv.

calendar itself; but it is difficult to believe that either
Spain or Gaul, lacking political and ecclesiastical
centralization, had developed any very strong tradition
of uniformity and fixity—as Rome had—before the
idea of 'heortological' variation began to operate.
Precisely when or where this happened, nobody
knows; almost certainly not in Rome, probably in
Gaul or Spain, where the intense veneration of the
Diocletian martyrs and their local cults would en-
courage its rapid development.[1] The earliest documen-
tary evidence of such variability comes from Marseilles.
There, about 450, the priest Musaeus is said to have
first chosen lections and responsories 'appropriate to
feast-days,' and then, a few years later, to have composed a large and excellent volume of Masses (*sacramentorum*), containing in separate sections the 'proper'
of 'offices and seasons,' the lections, and the psalms
arranged for singing—a work 'suitable in its entirety
for praying to God (*supplicandi Deo*) and acknowledg-
ing (*contestandi*) His benefits,' and exhibiting the 'deep
and disciplined eloquence' of its author.[2] What
variable formulas it comprised can only be conjec-
tured. The word 'contestandi' certainly suggests
contestationes, the Gallican proper prefaces; 'supplicandi'
might apply to any or all of the celebrant's prayers,
and pretty certainly it means more than the variable
Collect, Secret, and Post-Communion of the Roman
rite.

[1] The *Peristephanon* of Prudentius, written before 400, refers more than
once to the liturgical commemoration of the martyrs on their anniversaries.
[2] Gennadius, *De scriptoribus eccl.* lxxix (M.P.L. LVIII, 1103). About the
same time, Eusebius of Milan (d. 465) is traditionally credited with the
Ambrosian Proper Prefaces for the greater festivals.

From that time onward the composition of Masses becomes in Gaul and Spain—as nowhere else, so far as I know—a recognized literary activity. Sidonius Apollinaris, Bishop of Clermont Ferrand (d. *c.* 487), is the earliest known example in Gaul—and it is noteworthy that Gregory of Tours, nearly a century later, published a collection of the Masses of Sidonius;[1] they were evidently not out of date, whatever developments may have taken place in the meantime.[2] There must have been hundreds of such Masses written, and not only by bishops; Gregory says that even the unspeakable King Chilperic wrote 'hymns and Masses'—very badly.[3] But probably Spain, rather than Gaul, was the chief centre of liturgical composition in the sixth and seventh centuries, and Spanish texts quickly found their way over the Pyrenees. We have already noted one Gallican borrowing,[4] and many others may be seen in the *Missale Gothicum* and the Bobbio Missal; while there is little evidence, if any, that Spain returned the compliment.

Liturgical texts produced in this way could hardly fail to reflect current literary taste, and the Gallican 'stylus ecclesiasticus'[5] is as unlike the Roman as it could well be, but not unlike the mannered and 'euphuistic' prose of Sidonius and Avitus. In Gaul

---

[1] *Hist. franc.* II, xx. Gregory mentions this in connection with an occasion when Sidonius, having lost the 'libellum' which he was wont to use, extemporized a whole Mass with amazing eloquence. He evidently used no such 'egregium et non parvum volumen' as Musaeus had compiled.

[2] E.g. Avitus of Vienne, *c.* 515, 'instituit orandi modum' (*Ibid.* II, xxxiv).

[3] *Ibid.* VI, xlvi.   [4] See above, p. 20.

[5] The phrase is Gregory's (*Hist. franc.* VIII, xx), in reference to certain prayers composed in exile by Praetextatus of Rouen; they displeased some of his fellow-bishops 'quia artem secutus minime fuerat.'

itself, where this style probably began, it would seem to have kept within fairly reasonable bounds. There is nothing in the Masses of Mone,[1] and little in the later Gallican books, to compare with the extreme prolixity and artificiality of the contemporary Spanish productions, where all the rhetorical *schemata* of the textbooks[2] are in constant use, along with a tiresome habit of internal rhyme which is probably Gothic in origin. Here, for example, is the *Collectio* for Christmas Day from the *Missale Gothicum*,[3] a formula of quite normal length and style:

Deus, qui dives es in misericordia, qua mortuos nos peccatis, convivificasti Christo Filio tuo, ut formam servi acciperet, qui omnia formavit, ut qui erat in deitate generaretur in carne, ut involveretur in pannis qui adorabatur in stellis, ut jaceret in praesepio qui regnabat in caelo: invocantibus nobis aurem majestatis tuae propitiatus adcommoda, donans hoc per ineffabilem tuae misericordiae caritatem, ut qui exultamus de nativitate Filii tui, qui vel ex Virgine natus, vel ex Spiritu Sancto regeneratus est, pareamus praeceptis ejus, quibus nos edocuit ad salutem. Praesta per Dominum nostrum *etc*.

And here, for comparison, is the corresponding Spanish *Alia*,[4] equally typical:

Te, Domine Christe Ihesu, te Deum pluraliter homines salvantem, et hominem in Deo singulariter potentem invocamus, laudamus, rogamus: adsis ut parcas, miserearis, ignoscas. Des in corde vota quae compleas; des in ore verba quae exaudias; des in opere facta quae benedicas. Non petimus renovari nobis, sicut in hac die olim acta est, corporalem nativitatem tuam; sed petimus incorporari nobis invisibilem divinitatem tuam. Quod praestitum est carnaliter sed singulariter tunc Mariae, nunc spiritaliter praestetur Ecclesiae: ut te fides indubitata concipiat; te

---

[1] One of them—that of St. Germanus—is written in hexameters!
[2] E.g. Isidor, *Etymologiae*, I, xxxvi ff.
[3] M.P.L. LXXII, 227.   [4] *Lib. moz. sacr.*, 54.

mens de corruptione liberata parturiat; te semper anima virtute Altissimi obumbrata contineat. Ne discedas a nobis, sed procedas ex nobis. Sis revera Emmanuel noster, nobiscum Deus. Digneris manere in nobis, et pugnare pro nobis. Te enim pugnante, nos vincimus. Solve nos, quaesumus, pannis putribus peccatorum, qui te pro peccatis nostris dignatus es putredine ligari pannorum. Lac tuum Ecclesiae tuae parvulos nutriat. Adeo infirmos delicatus olerum cibus pascat, ut ad percipiendum fortiorem ac solidum cibum validiores quotidie vires crescant. Et ita noverimus defecatam voluntatem et fidem exhibere firmissimam, ut iugiter enitamur auxilio tuo ad vitam pervenire perfectam.

The desire to impress and edify, which underlies all this verbosity and 'fine writing,' may rank as a third Gallican characteristic. It comes out not only in the typical *Praefationes* (or *Missae*), which are exhortations addressed to the 'fratres carissimi,' and in the *Contestationes* (or *Illationes*—i.e. Proper Prefaces), where something of the sort, derived from their Syrian prototypes, is fairly general,[1] but also in the other formulas of the Mass, to the frequent detriment of their proper liturgical function. Not only are prayers overladen with didactic relative clauses, for the benefit of the congregation, but they tend to be concerned far more with the particular occasion, the commemorated festival or saint, than with the eucharistic rite itself. An *Ad pacem*, for example, may become—as in the Mass for St. Maurice and his Companions[2]—simply a prayer for the saints' intercessions. Or, more seriously, the vital reference to

---

[1] These formulas are sometimes based directly on sermons: e.g. the *Contestatio* for Maundy Thursday, in the *Missale Gothicum* (No. 209), on Augustine, *Tract. lv in Joh.*; that for the Assumption (No. 98), on the sermons of Ildefonsus of Toledo.

[2] *Missale Gothicum*, No. 422 (M.P.L. LXXII, 302).

the sacrifice of Christ—apart from the Institution formula—may almost or entirely disappear in a welter of hagiology and rhetoric. This happens so frequently in the Spanish texts that it may well explain the omission of the *Post mysterium* from most of the saint's day Masses in the *Missale Gothicum*. It certainly constitutes the gravest liturgical defect of the developed Gallican rite.

A fourth characteristic—later in development than the others—is the tendency to interpolate prayers not essential to the rite. These take two forms: (1) the so-called *apologiae*, and (2) prayers accompanying ritual acts originally performed in silence. The former is a seventh-century innovation; two specimens appear—one in the singular (headed *Post prophetiam*) and one in the plural (headed *Collectio*)—before the Mass of St. Germanus in Mone's collection.[1] A much longer and more elaborate example stands before the *Praefatio* of the Easter Mass in the *Missale Gothicum*; a few lines of it may be quoted:

Subveni ergo, subveni pietas ineffabilis. Ignosce, ignosce mihi, Trinitas mirabilis. Parce, parce, parce, supplico, Deitas placabilis. Exaudi, exaudi, exaudi me, rogo, his verbis illius Filii tui clamantem; Pater, aeterne Deus, peccavi in caelo et coram te; iam non sum dignus vocari filius tuus; fac me ut unum de mercenariis tuis.[2]

A considerable number of these 'prayers of humble access' appear later in Gallican supplements to the *Gregorianum*,[3] one of them figuring also in the Bobbio

---

[1] Mone, *op. cit.*, p. 37. Mone groups them separately, as 'Missa X'; but Wilmart includes them in the Mass of St. Germanus.
[2] No. 275. M.P.L. LXXII. 277.   [3] M.P.L. LXXVII, 229.

Missal[1] and (as an *Alia*) in the Spanish sacramentary, which is probably its source.[2]

The other sort of interpolated prayer, said silently in conjunction with some ritual action, is a still later development, and probably North Gallican in origin— not, that is, a feature of the traditional Gallican rite, although widely adopted throughout Gaul, and later taken over into the modern Roman rite. Of this sort are the vesting prayers, the celebrant's preparation, the private prayers at the offertory and the washing of hands, and those before the priest's Communion. The only example in the older books is the single *Collectio ad panis fractionem* in the *Missale Gothicum*.[3]

Finally, we may mention the characteristic Gallican fondness for honorific or symbolic ceremonial. We have already noted instances of this—the processions at the entrance, the Gospel, and the offertory, the lifting of the veil over the oblations during the prayers for the dead, the elaborate fraction of the Host—and many more could be adduced from the rites of Holy Week and other special functions, which we cannot now examine. Most of these ceremonies come from the East; it is the readiness to receive and adapt them

[1] No. 483. M.P.L. LXXII, 536.

[2] *Lib. moz. sacr.*, 513, 615. The *apologia* proper seems not to have been adopted in Spain. The formula 'Accedam ad te,' which the *Liber Ordinum* (col. 230) directs the priest to say silently at the altar before beginning the Mass, and which the modern missal places before the anaphora, is quite unlike the Gallican formulas. It is attributed to Julian of Toledo (d. 690), and may be originally a preparation for preaching (cf. F. Cabrol, in *D.A.C.L.*, art. 'Mozarabe'). Used in the Mass, it well indicates the habit of thinking of the liturgy in terms of edification.

[3] No. 272. M.P.L. LXXII, 277. There are, indeed, many prayers of this sort in the Missal of Ximenes, but they are late importations from Gaul, not found even in the eleventh century *Liber Ordinum*.

that is distinctively Gallican. Some of them, indeed, find their way at a later date into Roman use, along with other Gallican elements, but they remain easily distinguishable from the severely simple and practical Roman substratum; it is hardly too much to say that any ceremony in the modern Roman rite which is not strictly essential is Gallican in origin.

VII

THE DISAPPEARANCE OF THE RITE

Officially, the Gallican rite came to an end by order of Charlemagne, at the end of the eighth century. But it is doubtful if it could have been found in use, in anything like its pure form, for a long time before that, except perhaps in remote parishes of Burgundy or Septimania.[1] Charlemagne's youngest son, Charles the Bald, writes to the clergy of Ravenna that 'the Gallican churches differed from those of Rome and Milan in the celebration of the divine offices up to the time of our grandfather Pippin'[2]—i.e. Pippin the Short, who came to power as Mayor of the Palace over Neustria and Burgundy in 747, was elected King of all the Franks in 751, and died in 768. This is precisely the period which produced the romanized *Missale Gothicum* and *Gallicanum Vetus*, but it would be a profound mistake to suppose that it marked the beginning of Roman influence. These Gallican missals

[1] I.e. the coastal strip between the Rhone and the Pyrenees, which had been a province of Visigothic Spain up to the Moorish conquest.

[2] Mansi, *Concil. ampl. coll.* XVIII (para. 2), p. 730. The letter is not in the *Monumenta Germanicae Historiae*, and Mansi gives no source.

themselves certainly represent an archetype already romanized,[1] and in the north and east of France many manuscripts of the *Gelasianum*, with various Gallican additions, were in use before 700—perhaps even before 600.[2] By 750 it is probable that at least half the churches in Gaul were using the gallicanized Roman rite, and the rest the romanized Gallican rite. King Pippin could have had no hesitation in choosing to support the Romeward trend. Not only was his chief adviser in such matters the strongly pro-Roman St. Boniface, but also, in the risky business of assuming royal power, he had sought the approval of the Papacy, and had been solemnly crowned by Pope Stephen II on the occasion of the latter's visit to the French court in 753. Their collaboration issued in a general order to the French clergy to learn and use the 'cantum Romanum'—i.e. the whole Roman Office.[3] We know that this was done at Metz, under St. Chrodegang, about 754, and at Rouen a few years later; and about 760 Pippin received from Pope Paul copies of the Roman Antiphoner and Responsorial. Similar action would doubtless have been taken in regard to the Mass, but for the fact that no one in France possessed an authoritative text of the *Gregorianum*.

---

[1] Roman elements in the *Missale Gothicum* appear also in the fragmentary text edited by W. J. Anderson (*Jour. Theol. Studies*, XXIX, p. 338. July, 1928), probably from north or north-east France, and written about 750.

[2] The earliest known copy of the *Gelasianum*, written *c.* 700, comes from Paris, and contains Gallican elements.

[3] The original is not extant, but Charlemagne re-enacts the order in 789, in his *Admonitio generalis, cap. lxxx* (M.G.H., Leges, sect. II, t. I, pars prima): 'secundum quod beatae memoriae genitor noster Pippinus rex decertavit ut fieret, quando Gallicanum tulit, ob unanimitatem apostolicae sedis et sanctae Dei Ecclesiae pacificam concordiam.'

When Charlemagne, not without considerable difficulty and delay, had at last obtained this from Pope Hadrian about 790, the final step could be taken. The *Hadrianum* itself was in some respects inaccurate and incomplete, but the scholarly editorship of Alcuin put it into workable shape and added a supplement of votive Masses and other occasional rites for permissive use.[1] It was issued along with a royal 'Act of Uniformity' enjoying its adoption throughout the whole realm. Alcuin's supplement indeed contained much Gallican and Spanish material, recast to fit the Roman framework, and it is, of course, possible that some conservatives went on using the older rite or tried to revive it after Charlemagne's death, but to all intents and purposes his book brought the Gallican rite to an end. By 820 Amalarius of Metz says that every one in Gaul knew the King's book;[2] twenty-five years later Strabo says that it was everywhere used, with easily distinguishable additions.[3] And within another half-century Charles the Bald, in the letter already mentioned, says that he knows the rite of his forefathers because clergy from Toledo had come and celebrated the Mass in his presence according to the customs of that church[4]—an interesting indication, by

[1] The best edition of Alcuin's book is that of H. A. Wilson, for the Henry Bradshaw Society, 1915, under the title of *The Gregorian Sacramentary*.
[2] *De eccl. off.* I, xxxvii (M.P.L. CV, 1068).
[3] *De rebus eccl.* XXV (M.P.L. CXIV, 956).
[4] He had obviously invited them, as he did others from Jerusalem and Constantinople, who also performed their liturgies before him. There is a story, probably apocryphal, that Charlemagne, wishing to test the success of his reforms, expressed a desire to attend the Gallican rite, but that no one could be found who knew it except an old priest from Spain. D. Buenner, *L'ancienne liturgie romaine—Le rite Lyonnais* (Lyons, 1934), p. 60.

the way, that he knew of no distinction between the rites of Gaul and Spain.

It must not, of course, be supposed that Gaul maintained the pure Gregorian liturgy; Gauls remained Gallican. Other supplements besides Alcuin's appeared from time to time, and were also gradually amalgamated with the genuine Roman material, to produce eventually the hybrid sacramentaries which, under Popes of Germanic origin, established themselves in Rome itself. It is often said that the non-Roman elements in these—and therefore in the modern Roman missal—are 'Gallican'; but that must not be taken to imply that they come from the old Gallican rite. The Roman Pontifical and Ritual are indeed full of forms and ceremonies which do come from that rite, more or less directly; but the missal has borrowed little or nothing from it, except the processions of Candlemas and Palm Sunday, the blessings of candles, ashes, and palms, and some of the special rites of Holy Week. These are of secondary importance, but it may still rank as no small achievement of the Gallican genius to have given permanent liturgical expression to Christian devotion on the most sacred days of the Church's year.

BIBLIOGRAPHY

COLLECTIONS OF GALLICAN TEXTS

G. M. Tommasi, *Codices Sacramentorum Nongentis Annis Vetustiores* (Rome, 1680).

J. Mabillon, O.S.B., *De Liturgia Gallicana Libri Tres* (Rome, 1685; repr. in J. P. Migne, *P.L.* lxxii, cols. 99–448).

J. M. Neale–G. H. Forbes, *The Ancient Liturgies of the Gallican Church* (Burntisland, 1855–57).

Various fragments also printed in the new edition of the *Missale Gallicanum Vetus* by L. C. Mohlberg, O.S.B.–L. Eizenhöfer, O.S.B.–P. Siffrin, O.S.B., cited below.

BOBBIO MISSAL

Editio princeps in J. Mabillon, O.S.B., *Museum Italicum, seu Collectio Veterum Scriptorum ex Bibliothecis Italicis eruta* (Paris, 1687), i, pt. 2, pp. 278–397; repr. in J. P. Migne, *P.L.* lxxii, cols. 451–580.

Critical edition by E. A. Lowe, *The Bobbio Missal.* A Gallican Mass-Book (Henry Bradshaw Society liii [text] and lvii [facsimile], 1917–20). Notes by A. Wilmart, O.S.B., –E. A. Lowe–H. A. Wilson (Henry Bradshaw Society lxi, 1924).

MISSALE GOTHICUM

Editio princeps in G. M. Tommasi, *Codices Sacramentorum Nongentis Annis Vetustiores* (Rome, 1680), pp. 263–317.

J. Mabillon, O.S.B., *De Liturgia Gallicana Libri Tres* (Paris, 1865), pp. 188–300; repr. in J. P. Migne, *P.L.* lxxii, cols. 225–318.

Critical edition in H. M. Bannister, *Missale Gothicum.* A Gallican Sacramentary (Henry Bradshaw Society lii and liv, 1917–19).

Facsimile in C. Mohlberg, O.S.B., *Missale Gothicum.* Das gallikanische Sakramentar (Cod. Vat. Regin. 317) des VII.–VIII. Jahrhunderts (Augsburg, 1929).

MISSALE GALLICANUM VETUS

Editio princeps in G. M. Tommasi, *Codices Sacramentorum Nongentis Annis Vetustiores* (Rome, 1680), pp. 433–92.

J. Mabillon, O.S.B., *De Liturgia Gallicana Libri Tres* (Rome, 1685), pp. 329–78; repr. in J. P. Migne, *P.L.* lxxii, cols. 339–82.

Critical edition in L. C. Mohlberg, O.S.B.–L. Eizenhöfer, O.S.B.–P. Siffrin, O.S.B., *Missale Gallicanum Vetus* (Rerum Ecclesiasticarum Documenta cura Pontificii Athenaei Sancti Anselmi de Urbe edita, Series Maior, Fontes iii, Rome, 1958).

MISSALE FRANCORUM

Editio princeps in G. M. Tommasi, *Codices Sacramentorum Nongentis Annis Vetustiores* (Rome, 1680), pp. 348–431.

J. Mabillon, O.S.B., *De Liturgia Gallicana Libri Tres* (Paris, 1685), pp. 301–28; repr. in J. P. Migne, *P.L.* lxxii, cols. 317–40.

Critical edition in L. C. Mohlberg, O.S.B.–L. Eizenhöfer, O.S.B.–P. Siffrin, O.S.B., *Missale Francorum* (Rerum Ecclesiasticarum Documenta cura Pontificii Athenaei Sancti Anselmi de Urbe edita, Series Maior, Fontes ii, Rome, 1957).

MONE MASSES

Editio princeps in F. J. Mone, *Lateinische und griechische Messen aus dem zweiten bis sechsten Jahrhundert* (Frankfurt a.M., 1850; repr. in J. P. Migne, *P.L.* cxxxviii, cols. 862–82).

Critical edition in L. C. Mohlberg, O.S.B.–L. Eizenhöfer, O.S.B.–P. Siffrin, O.S.B., *Missale Gallicanum Vetus*, cited above, pp. 74–91.

PS.-GERMANUS OF PARIS

Letters printed in E. Martène, *Thesaurus Novus Anecdotorum* v (Paris, 1717), pp. 91–100; repr. in J. P. Migne, *P.L.* lxxii, cols. 89–98.

P. Batiffol, *Études de Liturgie et d'Archéologie Chrétienne* (1919), pp. 245–90 ('L'*Expositio Liturgiae Gallicanae* attribué à Saint Germain de Paris').

BIBLIOGRAPHY

A. Wilmart, O.S.B., in *D.A.C.L.* vi (pt. 1, 1924), cols. 1049–102, s.v. 'Germain de Paris (Lettres attribuées à Saint).'

LECTIONARIES ETC.

The Lectionary of Luxeuil was first publd. by J. Mabillon, O.S.B., *De Liturgia Gallicana Libri Tres* (Paris, 1685), pp. 106–73. P. Salmon, O.S.B., *Le Lectionnaire de Luxeuil* (Collectanea Biblica Latina vii, Rome, 1944 [text]; *ibid.* ix, 1953 [study]).

G. Morin, O.S.B., 'Le Lectionnaire de l'Église de Paris' in *Revue Bénédictine* x (1893), pp. 438–41.

D. de Bruyne, O.S.B., 'Les Notes Liturgiques du Manuscrit 134 de la Cathédrale de Trèves' in *Revue Bénédictine* xxxiii (1921), pp. 46–52.

A. Dold, O.S.B., *Das älteste Liturgiebuch der lateinischen Kirche.* Ein altgallikanisches Lektionar des 5/6 Jhs. aus dem Wolfenbütteler Palimpsest Weissenburgensis 76 (Texte und Arbeiten herausgegeben durch die Erzabtei Beuron I. Abt., Hefte 26–28; Beuron, 1936).

E. Chatelain, 'Fragments Palimpsestes d'un Lectionnaire Mérovingien' in *Revue d'Histoire et de Littérature Religieuses* v (1900), pp. 193–9.

G. Morin, O.S.B., 'Un Lectionnaire Mérovingien avec Fragments du Texte Occidental des Actes' in *Revue Bénédictine* xxv (1908), pp. 161–6.

A. Wilmart, O.S.B., 'Un Lectionnaire d'Aniane' in *Revue Mabillon* xiii (1923), pp. 40–53.

G. Morin, O.S.B., 'Notices d'Ancienne Littérature Chrétienne, 6, Les Notes Liturgiques du Manuscrit Vat. Regin. Lat. 9' in *Revue Bénédictine* xv (1898), pp. 104–6.

G. Morin, O.S.B., 'Fragments Inédits et jusqu'à Présent Uniques d'Antiphonaire Gallican' in *Revue Bénédictine* xxii (1905), pp. 329–56.

G. Morin, O.S.B., 'Un Recueil Gallican Inédit de *Benedictiones Episcopales* en Usage à Freising aux VIIe–IXe Siècles' in *Revue Bénédictine* xxix (1912), pp. 168–94.

STUDIES

J. Mabillon, O.S.B., *De Liturgia Gallicana Libri Tres* (Paris, 1685), esp. pp. 1–96.

J. M. Neale–G. H. Forbes, *The Ancient Liturgies of the Gallican Church* (Burntisland, 1855–57).

L. Duchesne, *Origines du Culte Chrétien* (1889), pp. 81–99, 143–51, 180–217.

R. Buchwald, *De Liturgia Gallicana* (Dissertation, Breslau, 1890).

[P. Cagin, O.S.B.,] *Antiphonarium Ambrosianum* (*Paléographie Musicale* v, Solesmes, 1896).

L. Duchesne, 'Sur l'Origine de la Liturgie Gallicane' in *Revue d'Histoire et de Littérature Religieuses* v (1900), pp. 31–47 [discussion of preceding item of P. Cagin.]

G. Mercati, *Antiche Reliquie Liturgiche* (Studi e Testi vii, 1902), esp. pp. 72–5 ('Sull'Origine della Liturgia Gallicana').

H. Leclercq, O.S.B., in *D.A.C.L.* vi (pt. 1; 1924), cols. 473–596, s.v. 'Gallicane (Liturgie).'

J. B. Thibaut, A.A., *L'Ancienne Liturgie Gallicane. Son Origine et sa Formation en Provence aux Ve et VIe Siècles* (Paris, 1929).

F. Cabrol, O.S.B., 'Les Origines de la Liturgie Gallicane' in *Revue d'Histoire Ecclésiastique* xxvi (1930), pp. 951–62.

F. Cabrol, O.S.B., in R. Aigrain (ed.), *Liturgia*. Encyclopédie populaire des Connaissances Liturgiques (Paris, 1931), pp. 793–800.

T. Klauser, 'Die liturgischen Austauschbeziehungen zwischen der römischen und der fränkisch-deutschen Kirche vom achten bis zum elften Jahrhundert' in *Historisches Jahrbuch* liii (1933), pp. 169–89.

M. Righetti, *Storia Liturgica* i (Milan, ed. 2, 1950), pp. 123–39.

E. Griffe, 'Aux Origines de la Liturgie Gallicane' in *Bulletin de Littérature Ecclésiastique* lii (1951), pp. 17–43.

A. Baumstark, *Comparative Liturgy* (Eng. ed. by F. L. Cross, 1958), esp. pp. 209–12.

Mozarabic Books

These include:

[A. Ortiz,] *Missale Mixtum secundum Regulam Beati Isidori dictum Mozarabes* (Toledo, 1500). Revised edition by A. Lesley, S.J., *Missale Mixtum secundum Regulum Beati Isidori dictum Mosarabes* (Rome, 1755; repr. *ibid.*, 1804, and Toledo, 1875; also in J. P. Migne, *P.L.* lxxxv).

[A. Ortiz,] *Breviarium secundum Regulam Beati Isidori* (Toledo, 1502). Revised edition by A. Lorenzo, *Breviarium Gothicum secundum Regulam Beatissimi Isidori* (Madrid, 1775; repr. Rome, 1804, and Toledo, 1875; also in J. P. Migne, *P.L.* lxxxvi).

M. Férotin, O.S.B., *Le Liber Ordinum en Usage dans l'Église Wisigothique et Mozarabe d'Espagne du Cinquième au Onzième Siècle* (Monumenta Ecclesiae Liturgica ed. F. Cabrol, O.S.B. –H. Leclercq, O.S.B., v; Paris, 1904).

M. Férotin, O.S.B., *Le Liber Mozarabicus Sacramentorum et les Manuscrits Mozarabes* (Monumenta Ecclesiae Liturgica ed. F. Cabrol, O.S.B.–H. Leclercq, O.S.B., vi; Paris, 1912).

G. Morin, O.S.B., *Liber Comicus sive Lectionarius Missae quo Toletana Ecclesia ante Annos Mille et Ducentos Utebatur* (Anecdota Maredsolana i; Maredsous, 1893).

Benedictines of Silos, *Antiphonarium Mozarabicum de la Catedral de León* (León, 1928).

J. Vives, *Oracional Visigòtico* (Barcelona, 1946).

INDEX